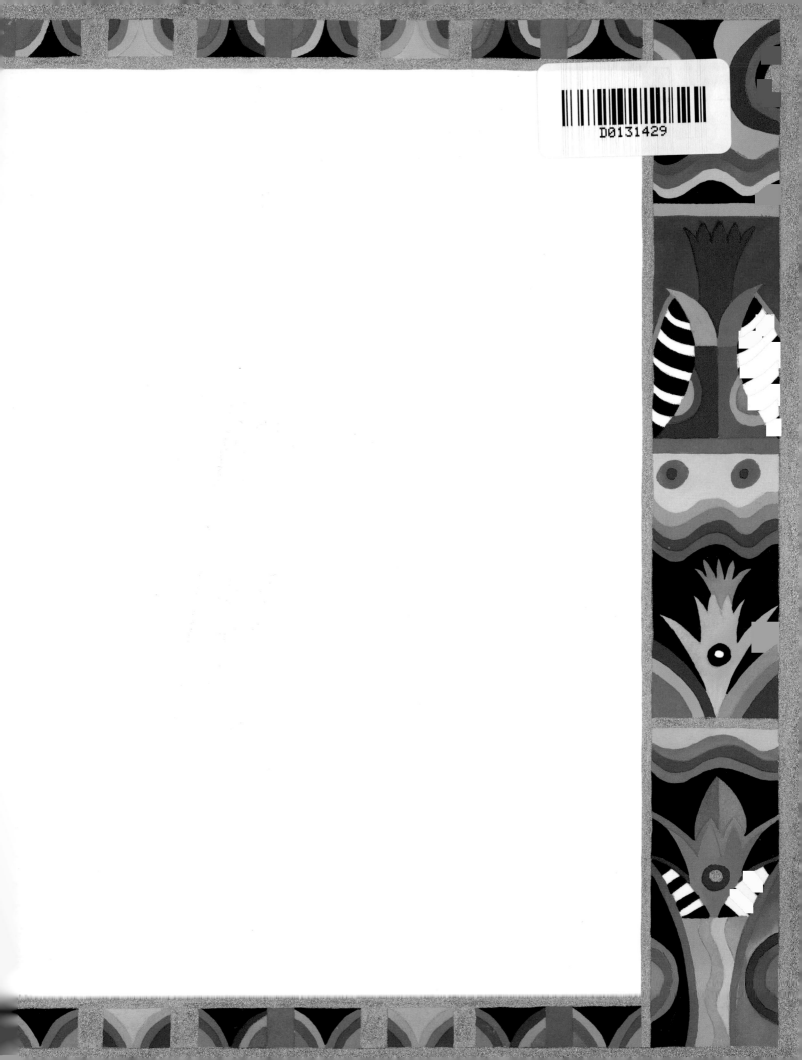

For Robyn – C.J.M.

For Sean-George, Billie-George and Crouch – C.B.

KINGFISHER
Larousse Kingfisher Chambers Inc.
95 Madison Avenue
New York, New York 10016

First American edition 1996
2 4 6 8 10 9 7 5 3 1

First published in Great Britain in 1996 by
Frances Lincoln Limited, 4 Torriano Mews
Torriano Avenue, London NW5 2RZ

LIBRARY OF CONGRESS CATALOGING-IN-PUBLICATION DATA
Moore, C.J.
Ishtar and Tammuz: a Babylonian myth of the seasons / C.J. Moore,
Christina Balit. -- 1st American ed.
p.   cm.
Summary: A retelling of the Babylonian myth telling how the death
of Ishtar's son Tammuz brings about the changing seasons on earth.
1. Inanna (Sumerian deity) -- Juvenile literature. 2. Mythology,
Assyro-Babylonian -- Juvenile literature. 3. Seasons -- Mythology
-- Juvenile literature.   [1. Mythology, Assyro-Babylonion.
2. Seasons -- Mythology.]   I. Balit, Christina. II. Title.
BL 160B.18M68   1996
398.2'0935'01 -- dc20   96-33944   CIP   AC

ISBN 0-7534-5012-7

Printed in Hong Kong

ISHTAR AND TAMMUZ

A Babylonian Myth of the Seasons

Adapted and retold by Christopher Moore
Illustrated by Christina Balit

Kingfisher
NEW YORK

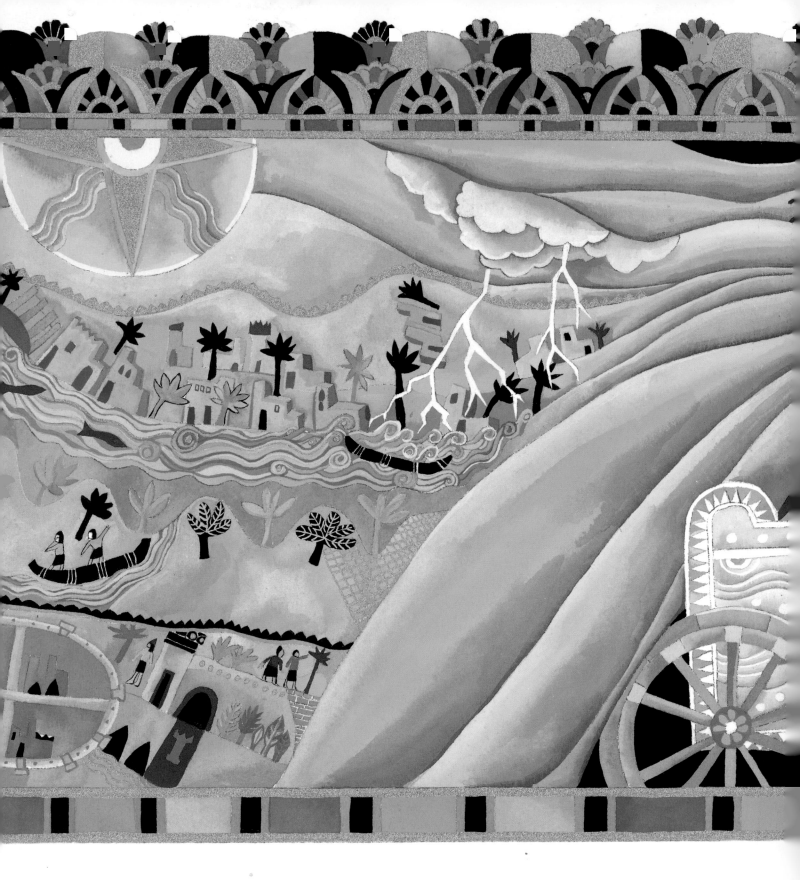

In long ago Babylon, four thousand years past, Ishtar was worshiped as queen of the stars and goddess of all creation. No being was more beautiful, more powerful, or more terrible.

Ishtar held the power of life and death over all. Sometimes she brought storms, hail, and thunder down upon the earth. Sometimes, in her darker moods, she brought down the terror and destruction of war.

Ishtar sent her son, Tammuz, to live on the earth.

Wherever he walked, the earth brought forth fruit and crops and the green of the land. The birds and animals followed the sound of his flute for sheer joy, and the people welcomed him and loved him dearly. They called him the Green One.

From the heavens above, Ishtar watched her son and was content.

But as time passed, Ishtar began to feel that Tammuz was adored too much, and that his power was rivaling her own. Her heart hardened, and calling her messengers of war and terror, she ordered them to kill Tammuz.

Ishtar's servants struck Tammuz down with their curved swords. The sun hid its face as the young man's blood ran down and seeped into the earth.

Tammuz descended to the dark underworld, the home of the dead, where Allatu, Ishtar's sister, ruled. Allatu welcomed him with grim pleasure, for she hated her sister who lived in the light of the sun.

On the upper earth, after the death of Tammuz, all growing things withered and died. The crops and grasses shriveled, leaves curled and fell. The birds fell silent and the earth grew barren.

With Tammuz gone, a dull sadness came upon the world.
As the rivers and springs ran dry, hunger and thirst followed.
The unhappy people cried out to Ishtar and, as each day passed,
their prayers grew more desperate.

Finally, Ishtar heard their prayers. When she came down to the earth she found the trees bare, the meadows without grass or flowers, the birds huddled and silent. She saw the sad, tired faces of the people and heard their laments. She saw their offerings upon the altar of Tammuz, the clouds of incense, and the uplifted arms of the priestess.

"Ishtar, Queen of Heaven," cried the priestess, "Be merciful and let Tammuz walk again among us. He is the green spirit of the land, the source of breath and birth." The priestess set fire to the offerings and the smoke rose into the sky.

Ishtar's heart was touched with pity. She spread her robe over the people and whispered into their hearts what she would do: she would go down to the kingdom of Allatu and do battle for Tammuz with her sister. Drawing on all her strength and powers, she began to descend to the realm of darkness.

As she departed, the upper earth became chill as winter. It was as if love itself had left creation.

Down and down Ishtar went, until at last she came to the cold grim city of the dead with its seven walls and seven gates where her sister ruled.

At the sight of this forbidding place, her courage almost failed her. No living thing, she knew, had ever returned from Allatu's realm. But she thought of Tammuz, and was filled with the strength of her love for him.

At the first gate, Ishtar called out to the watchman, "I am Ishtar, queen and goddess. Open so that I may pass!"

The watchman replied, "Give up your crown and you may pass. It is Allatu's command." Ishtar was furious, but she had no choice except to obey.

At the second gate, she was made to surrender the necklace of beads at her throat, the symbol of her power over the night heavens.

At the third gate, she had to give up her pendant earrings. But she thought still of Tammuz, and went on.

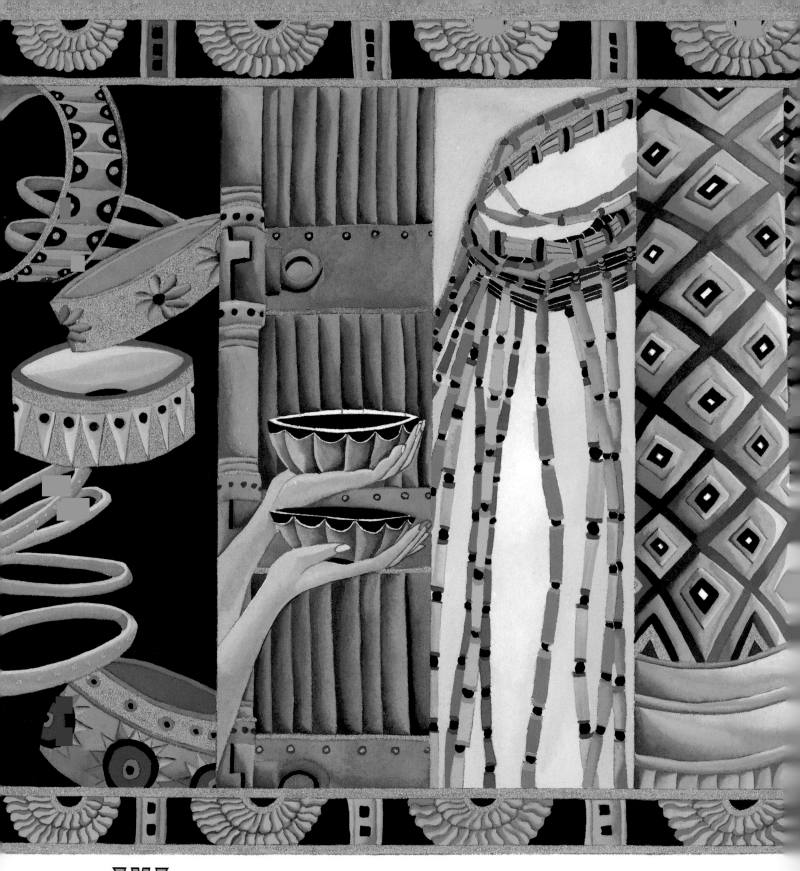

When she came to the fourth gate, Ishtar's bracelets of gold were taken from her wrists and ankles.

At the fifth gate, she had to surrender the jewels from her breast.

At the sixth gate, she put off her girdle of birthstones.

At the seventh and last gate, she had to leave her silken gown.

As she passed through the gates, one by one, she heard each grim door being shut and bolted behind her.

So, stripped of all her royal splendor and powers, Ishtar entered the very heart of the citadel.

Allatu, goddess of the underworld, half-woman, half-lioness, sat upon her jeweled throne surrounded by snakes and salamanders.

She laughed triumphantly to see Ishtar come defenseless before her. Beside the throne, Tammuz sat as if half asleep. He did not seem to recognize his mother.

Ishtar stood before Allatu and bowed her head. Then she fell on her knees and pleaded with her sister for Tammuz. But Allatu only laughed at her.

"Let me at least touch my beloved son," cried Ishtar.

"No!" screamed Allatu in fury—but too late, for Ishtar had leaped past the guardians of the throne to the side of Tammuz, and was embracing her son, the tears streaming from her eyes.

athed in Ishtar's warm tears, Tammuz felt the waters of life touching him once more. He awoke, and clung to his mother so closely that Allatu's guards could not separate them.

"Take him!" cried Allatu bitterly. "But do not think you have overcome my powers. You may both leave my realm, but on one condition—Tammuz must return to me for six months every year."

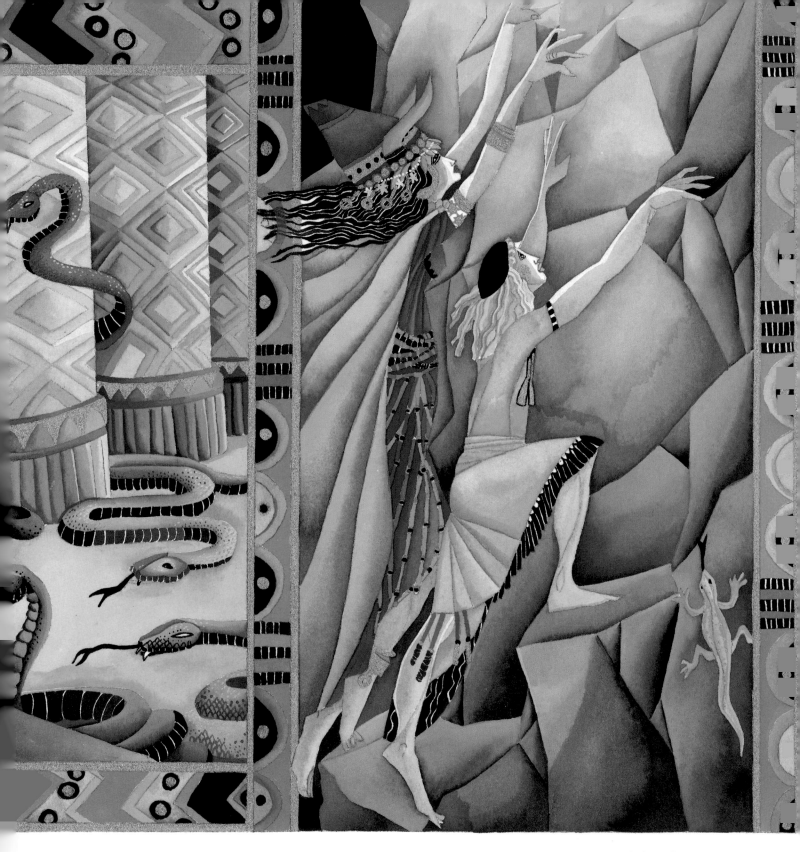

Ishtar and Tammuz had to agree. Together they hurried back through the seven great gates. One by one, Ishtar's queenly gown and jewels were restored to her until she stood, crowned once more, outside the realm of the dead. Then mother and son climbed through the dark caverns toward the upper earth.

When Tammuz stepped out onto the earth above, he kissed the ground for joy. Warmth and new life poured into all creation, song rose in the throats of the birds, and the animals broke from their deep sleep.

From this time on, so it would be each year. When Tammuz was summoned back to the underworld, cold winter descended on the land for six months.

But with his return each spring, nature woke again with joy, the trees felt the pulse of new sap and every seed in the ground stirred. Among the people a new liveliness was born. Dance and music filled the houses, and in every farm, village, town, and city, thankful prayers were offered for the return of Ishtar's beloved son, Tammuz.

To the people of ancient Mesopotamia (now Syria and Iraq) who grew crops and grazed their herds on the fertile plains of the Tigris and Euphrates rivers, the goodwill and the blessings of the Earth goddess Ishtar were all important.

Ishtar loved the semi-divine shepherd-king Tammuz. Early myths say their marriage ensured that the earth remained fruitful, but the great epic of Gilgamesh tells how Ishtar's power destroyed Tammuz. In one version of the story, Ishtar descended to the underworld to find him and was allowed to return from the underworld so long as Tammuz spent half the year there in her place.

For this simplified retelling I have made Tammuz the son of Ishtar, as he is often called "my son" in the ancient laments of Ishtar. The name Tammuz comes from an earlier form, Dumuzi, meaning "faithful son."

A similar mythical account of nature's yearly cycle— summer harvest followed by barren winter—can be found in the more familiar Greek myth of Demeter and Persephone. But this earlier story of Ishtar and her beloved Tammuz, with its origins some 5,000 years before Christ, reminds us of the close bond that we have to keep with nature and its cycles of life.